THE
K I D'S
GUIDE TO
NEW YORK CITY

2nd
edition

Eileen Ogintz

D1044297

gpp®
travel

Guilford, Connecticut

Special thanks to my daughter Regina Yemma for her research help.

All the information in this guidebook is subject to change. We recommend that you call ahead to obtain current information before traveling.

To buy books in quantity for corporate use or incentives, call **(800) 962-0973** or e-mail **premiums@GlobePequot.com**.

Editor: Amy Lyons
Project Editor: Lynn Zelem
Layout: Maggie Peterson
Text Design: Sheryl Kober
Illustrations licensed by Shutterstock.com

ISSN 1549-4276
ISBN 978-0-7627-7995-6

Printed in the United States of America
10 9 8 7 6 5 4 3 2 1

Contents

1 Say Hello to the Big Apple! 1

2 New York City's Neighborhoods 11

3 Dinosaurs, Fighter Jets, Mummies & Picasso 25

4 Play Ball! 39

5 Grab the Camera 49

6 Lady Liberty & Ellis Island 65

7 Eggrolls, Pizza, Giant Balloons & Bargains 79

8 Horns, Drums, Songs & More! 91

9 Monkeys, Elephants, Polar Bears &
   Alice in Wonderland 99

10 Ground Zero 109

   What a Trip! 117

   Index 121

1

Say Hello to the Big Apple!

Ready to take a big bite out of the Big Apple?

This city is so big that whatever you like—baseball or basketball, theater or art museums, dinosaurs or lions, playgrounds or stores, Chinese food or pizza—you'll find it here. And it will be great.

Check out all the big buildings. This is one place you won't get bored. In fact, there's so much to do it's impossible to do it all no matter how long you stay.

That's why New York is always tops on kids' lists of places they want to visit. You're lucky to be here. But New York is also home to millions of parents and kids. Many of them have come from around the world to live here. You probably haven't seen so many different kinds of people speak so many languages anywhere—the experts say

A NYC KID SAYS:
"I've got friends who are Chinese, Korean, Puerto Rican, Mexican, African American, Jewish, Indian . . . and a lot of others too."
—Regan, 11, NYC

{ **What's Cool?** You can always find something to eat—right on the street. New York kids love hot dogs from the street vendors you'll see everywhere (eat one New York-style with sauerkraut and mustard) and big soft hot pretzels. You'll also see vendors and trucks selling kabobs, ice cream, cupcakes, and Italian ice. Take your pick . . .

How Did New York Get Its Name?

The Algonquin Indians and other tribes were the first New Yorkers, here when Henry Hudson showed up in 1609. He was actually looking for a passageway to the Orient when he stumbled into New York Harbor. Fifteen years later, the Dutch had settled here and named the area New Amsterdam. But by 1674, the English were in charge, and they renamed the busy settlement New York after James, Duke of York.

A NYC KID SAYS:
"You can see the bridge and boats and water from my house. When it's dark outside, the bridge lights up too. It's super cool!"
—Jenna, 9, NYC

160 different ones, everything from Arabic to Spanish to Chinese. No matter what they wear or what language they speak, they're all still New Yorkers.

New Yorkers love their city and they want you to love it too.

{ **What's Cool?** You might be able to be on TV if you get up really early and hold up a funny sign outside a broadcasting studio. Head to NBC's Studios at Rockefeller Center (just off Fifth Avenue between 49th and 50th Streets) to join the crowd at *The Today Show.* You can join the crowd at *Good Morning America* at 42nd Street and Broadway.

Ask a New York kid on his way to school or in a museum to point you to the nearest playground or place to get a bagel.

So where do you want to go first? *The Kid's Guide to New York City* helps

A NYC KID SAYS:
"My dad plays softball in the park and we go and watch him play. I like how you can see the buildings when you're standing in the grass."
—Molly, 9, NYC

4

you have the most fun! We've asked New York City kids to help too. You'll see their ideas in every chapter.

GOT A MAP?

Manhattan is split into the East Side and the West Side by Fifth Avenue. You'll hear people talk about the Upper East Side and Upper West Side (where a lot of New Yorkers live) as if they were different countries! It's easy to understand New York if you think of it as a lot of little neighborhoods. Some New Yorkers hardly ever leave their own neighborhoods. You'll also hear some other funny names of neighborhoods, and if you know what they mean, you're on your way to becoming a New Yorker! In the next chapter we will go over some of the neighborhoods!

Pick places within one neighborhood to explore at one time. Your feet won't get nearly so tired!

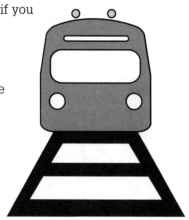

SUBWAYS & BUSES

Got comfy shoes? The best way to get around NYC is on foot—or on public transportation. Subways are the quickest—the first subway car is always the most fun—but you can see where you're going on the bus. Make sure you've

What's Cool? All the weird outfits you'll see on the streets. Draw the craziest one you've seen so far.

got a yellow **MetroCard** to pay for your ride. Check out the big subway maps that are posted in every train station. Grab a pocket map—also found at any train station—or check out www.mta.info and click on "Trip Planner." Check out the tile walls along some of the platforms— they're often the work of local artists.

DID YOU KNOW?

To hail a taxi, tell your parents to stand next to the curb and wave really hard. Don't forget to buckle your seatbelt when you get inside and ask the cabbie where he's from. Chances are it's some faraway country.

People in New York speak more than 160 languages!

The Dutch bought Manhattan Island from the Indians in 1626 for about $24 worth of tools and necklaces. See what you can buy in NYC today for $24.

- Leave lots of time to explore the city's neighborhoods as well as museums! That's where you'll discover the real New York—from coffee shops and delis to playgrounds and firehouses. Stop by a firehouse. New York firefighters will be glad to show you around—if they're not off fighting a fire!

- To make sure each member of the family picks out where you're going and what you're doing each day.

I ♥ NY

A VISITING KID SAYS:
"My favorite thing to do in NYC is travel around the city and window-shop."
—Brendan, 13, ME

2

New York City's Neighborhoods

Get your sneakers on!

The best way to see the way kids live in New York is to walk around the city's neighborhoods. And you'll want to wear your comfiest shoes.

Some kids spend all of their time in their own neighborhood, even though they live in such a big city. Ask kids you see to point you to their favorite playground or pizza place in the neighborhood. They'll know—just like you would at home.

Even if you get to stroll through just one or two city neighborhoods, you'll realize New York is a lot more than skyscrapers, restaurants, and big stores. You'll also hear some of the funny names for the neighborhoods, and once you know what they mean, you're on your way to becoming a New Yorker. What name do you think is the best?

- Alphabet City is named for avenues A, B, C, and D.

- Chelsea was named after a fancy neighborhood in London.

- Chinatown has become the biggest Asian community in North America.

DID YOU KNOW?
The **ferry to Staten Island** is free, and it's a great way to take in the view of the NYC skyline. Check out www.siferry.com for the schedule.

- **Flatiron District** is named after the building on Broadway and 23rd Street whose top looks like an old-fashioned iron.

- **Greenwich Village** started out as a 17th-century suburb, a green village. Today it's full of people, cafes, clubs, shops, and New York University.

- **Ground Zero** is the area of Lower Manhattan destroyed when the terrorists rammed the World Trade Center towers. Plans are in the works for new buildings. The National September 11 Memorial was opened to the public on September 12, 2011.

- **Harlem** is north of 110th Street and has long been a hub of New York's African-American community. Former President Bill Clinton has his offices here now.

- **Little Italy** is home to many Italian Americans and the site of some great Italian restaurants.

- **Lower East Side,** once the center of Jewish life in New York, now is known for its stores and shopping deals. This is one part of New York where you can still bargain!

- **Midtown** is just what it sounds like—the middle of town where there are lots of skyscrapers, restaurants, businesses, and stores.

- **Nolita** means "North of Little Italy" and that's where this trendy neighborhood is located.

- **SoHo** means South of Houston Street. (New Yorkers pronounce it "HOW-ston.") It has lots of art galleries and stores. You might want to stop in at the **New York**

DID YOU KNOW?
More than 1.6 million people live on Manhattan Island. That's more than live in all of Rhode Island.

City Fire Museum
(278 Spring St.; 212-691-1303; http://nycfiremuseum.org) while you're in the neighborhood to see how New York firemen have always done their jobs and the old hand-pulled and horse-drawn engines they used in the old days.

A VISITING KID SAYS:
"People are a lot nicer here than I thought they'd be."
—Nicholas, 13, Toronto, Canada

DID YOU KNOW?
You can walk or bike from Manhattan to Brooklyn across the Brooklyn Bridge. It's about a mile. The bridge took 16 years to build in the late 1800s.

- Times Square at 42nd Street and Broadway is the heart of the theater district—and the newest, hottest tourist area in the city—especially for kids.

- TriBeCa, on the Lower West Side, is short for "Triangle Below Canal (Street)."

- **Upper East Side** (North of 59th Street and east of Central Park) has some of New York's fanciest apartment buildings as well as a lot of shopping at stores such as Bloomingdale's.

- **Upper West Side** (North of 59th Street and everything west of Central Park) is the area that includes the American Museum of Natural History, a kids' favorite.

A lot of kids who visit New York also like to head downtown, especially to eat, shop, and people-watch. Many families live downtown too.

Greenwich Village—a lot of people just call it "The Village"—has lots of little stores, cafes, parks, and New York University. You'll see a lot of students in Washington Square Park and parents with kids who live in the neighborhood.

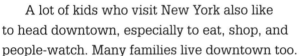

A VISITING KID SAYS:
"Eat hot, roasted nuts from a vendor. They're really good!"
—Alex, 9, NJ

If you love sports, head toward the Hudson River, and in between 17th and 23rd Streets you'll find the **Chelsea Piers Sports and Entertainment Complex** (www.chelseapiers .com). The complex is on four different historic

DID YOU KNOW?

Kids in NYC public schools speak more than 160 languages.

The name Manhattan comes from a Native American word that means "the place of hills."

piers over the river, and you can take your pick from 17 different sports to play, from rock climbing to ice-skating to sailing to soccer and more!

A NYC KID SAYS:
"My favorite thing to do in NY is play soccer in Riverside Park."
—Regan, 11, NYC

Very close to the piers is **The High Line** (www.thehigh line.org), a park built on top of old New York City freight train tracks. The park runs from Gansevoort Street in the Meatpacking District to 23rd Street, between 10th and 11th Avenues. This is a great place to visit and see the city from up in the air!

Head south of the Village for more shopping and eating in SoHo, Little Italy, Chinatown, and the Lower East Side, once the biggest Jewish community in the world.

Stop in at the **Lower East Side Tenement Museum** (108 Orchard St.; 212-982-8420; www.tenement.org) while you're in the neighborhood to see how kids lived when they were part of immigrant families 100 years ago. The museum is housed in an old tenement apartment building so you can see what it was like for families who lived and worked here. The apartments are so tiny!

It's still hard for all the kids who move to New York every year from other countries with their families—from Asia, Africa, India, the Caribbean Islands, and Central America, among other places. We're all really glad they've come. They're part of what makes New York so great.

How many languages did you hear today?

DID YOU KNOW?

The Bronx is the only one of New York's five boroughs connected to the mainland. To get to Manhattan, Queens, Staten Island, or Brooklyn you have to take a tunnel or a bridge.

Most NYC neighborhoods are only about 10 square blocks. They've got ice cream shops, pizza parlors, parks, schools, and lots of families and pets.

For some kids, their apartment building is like your block at home. They play with kids in their building and make friends with the doorman whose job it is to keep track of who goes in and out. They also go trick-or-treating in their building on Halloween!

- Big Apple Greeter (212-669-8159; www.bigapple greeter.org) offers FREE tours to visiting families and gives you all their top picks in their favorite neighborhoods. You need to make an appointment several weeks in advance.

- You want to take official yellow New York City taxis. Watch for cabs that have the light on the roof. If the light is on, the taxi is available. Raise your arm and wave it until the driver stops—hopefully!

- Time Out New York Kids (http://timeoutnewyork kids.com) has a list of current kid-friendly events.

- The City of New York Parks and Recreation (www .nycgovparks.org) can tell you where to find play-grounds, basketball courts, skating rinks, and more around the city.

{ What's Cool? Bargaining with vendors on the Lower East Side for everything from purses to T-shirts to sunglasses.

Stories Everywhere!

There are NYC libraries (www.nypl.org) all over the city, and in them you'll find many stories that take place in New York. Do you have a favorite? Here are some that NYC librarians think you'd like:

The Adventures of Taxi Dog by Debra and Sal Barracca

Eloise by Kay Thompson, the story of a 6-year-old who grows up in the Plaza Hotel

Lyle, Lyle Crocodile by Bernard Waber is about a NYC family who find a crocodile named Lyle in their bathtub!

The Cricket in Times Square by George Selden follows the adventures of a cricket who ends up in Times Square.

Stuart Little by E.B. White is the story of a NYC family's little mouse and takes place all around Central Park.

Harriet the Spy by Louise Fitzhugh follows the adventures of a sixth grader who lives in Manhattan.

From the Mixed-up Files of Mrs. Basil E. Frankweiler by E.L. Konigsburg tells the story of two Connecticut kids who camp out in the Metropolitan Museum and solve a mystery.

What's your favorite book set in New York?

_____

_____

_____

_____

_____

Movies Everywhere!

Lots of movies and TV shows are set in NYC and many are filmed here. Just a few of them include:

Spider-Man
Superman
Batman
Home Alone 2
Miracle on 34th Street
Ghostbusters
Stepmom
Stuart Little
Sesame Street

How many other New York–based movies can you name?

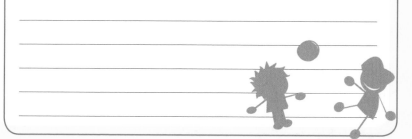

Harlem

More than a third of the length of Manhattan is north of 110th Street and that includes Harlem. First settled in the 1600s by Dutch tobacco farmers, Harlem in the 1920s was the most famous black community in the country, maybe in the world. Many African Americans still live there, and it's fast becoming a hot neighborhood again with new stores, restaurants, and attractions. Think you want to be a star? The **Apollo Theater** at 253 125th Street in Harlem has started to hold "amateur nights" to find new stars (for more information, visit www.apollotheater.org). If you're a dancer, you might want to see a performance at the **Dance Theatre of Harlem** (466 West 152nd St.; 212-690-2800; http://dance theatreofharlem.org).

A NYC KID SAYS:
"There are lots of places where you can do all the things you like to do at home, like Rollerblade, play tennis, go to the playground or the movies . . ."
—Alexa, 8, NYC

WORD SEARCH

Find some of the neighborhoods and boroughs of NYC
(Words are horizontal, vertical, and diagonal.)

Brooklyn
Chinatown
Greenwich
 Village
Ground Zero
Harlem

Little Italy
Lower East Side
Manhattan
Midtown
Queens
SoHo

Staten Island
The Bronx
Times Square
TriBeCa

```
S  T  S  M  U  X  O  M  D  S  D  X  Y  R  J  E  N
T  I  O  A  A  H  E  M  S  N  T  L  W  K  G  T  B
A  M  T  N  J  L  S  G  P  Y  A  B  Z  A  D  H  R
T  E  G  H  R  V  O  W  F  T  V  L  L  W  J  E  O
E  S  K  A  Q  T  H  P  I  W  R  L  S  N  Z  B  O
N  S  H  T  Z  M  O  E  E  J  I  B  D  I  O  R  K
I  Q  I  T  J  H  L  S  F  V  X  Y  N  S  N  O  L
S  U  E  A  Z  T  L  R  H  H  R  L  X  R  T  N  Y
L  A  V  N  T  E  K  C  Z  V  T  G  H  L  R  X  N
A  R  E  I  W  K  I  G  R  O  U  N  D  Z  E  R  O
N  E  L  E  X  W  Z  E  A  F  O  H  R  N  N  X  J
D  M  R  E  N  E  D  I  S  M  I  D  T  O  W  N  Q
H  I  H  E  M  C  H  I  N  A  T  O  W  N  E  Q  U
C  T  E  V  L  O  W  E  R  E  A  S  T  S  I  D  E
G  R  N  T  R  C  L  W  T  X  N  V  U  H  Q  W  E
G  K  T  D  T  R  I  B  E  C  A  Q  I  M  X  O  N
U  N  S  P  U  O  D  W  K  B  R  N  S  F  B  R  S
```

See page 123 for the answer key.

3
Dinosaurs, Fighter Jets, Mummies & Picasso

Name the place in New York

where you can time travel from ancient Egypt to Japan, from Europe hundreds of years ago to the US today.

Stumped? The answer is **The Metropolitan Museum of Art** (Fifth Avenue and 82nd Street; 212-535-7710; www .metmuseum.org). It's so big that from end to end, the museum stretches four New York City blocks—a quarter of a mile! There are more than 90 bathrooms!

The Met, as New Yorkers call it, has been around for more than 130 years. When you walk in the enormous front doors, you're entering one of the biggest and best art museums in the world. And even if you think you hate museums, this one can be fun as long as you know where to go. Of course, you can't possibly see everything in one visit!

DID YOU KNOW?

The **American Museum of Natural History** has a special website just for kids with activities and fun facts about science and the exhibits you can see at the museum. To find out about fossils, share discoveries with the scientists who made them, and more, visit: www.amnh.org/ology.

The Met has special family guides to the museum that you can download from its website, www.metmuseum .org, or you can pick them up at the information desk when you arrive.

And when you get tired, you can run and play all you want in Central Park just outside.

A lot of kids head for the ancient Egyptian Temple of Dendur first. In fact, it's one of the most popular exhibits in the entire museum.

A VISITING KID SAYS:
"Don't miss the Museum of Natural History. It's got lots of cool stuff."
—Rachel, 12, NJ

The temple, built in 15 BC, was taken apart in Egypt and transported by ship to New York. Engineers had to make detailed drawings so they would know how to put it back together to match how it appeared on the banks of the Nile River. If it had not been moved, it would have been covered by waters rising behind a new dam that was being built. The government of Egypt was very happy the temple could be brought to New York and gave it to our government as a present. The Met built an entire area to house the temple.

Kids also like to see the mummies that are in galleries in the main building near the Temple of Dendur. Thirteen of the mummies contain bodies, 12 of them adults and one child. We know that because museum experts did scans— similar to X-rays—of the mummies.

Have you ever imagined being a Knight in Shining Armor, fighting battles with a big sword? You might not want to after you stop to see the Met's collection of Arms and Armor. Those suits were heavy! So were the weapons!

Girls especially like the Costume Institute. You can see the kind of clothes people wore in different countries and a long time ago.

Of course, you're not going to leave without seeing some paintings and sculptures. Take your pick—Impressionist art from France, sculptures from the US, African masks, or Chinese porcelain. What part of the world do you want to visit today?

A NYC KIDS SAYS:
"Travel to the different boroughs to see what New York is really like."
—Jessica, 16, Brooklyn

THINK DINOSAURS. LOTS OF THEM!

The **American Museum of Natural History** (Central Park West at 79th Street; 212-769-5100; www.amnh.org) is home to one of the largest collections of vertebrate fossils—nearly one million in all!

This museum is the first one that many New York kids come to, and they return again and again. It's been here for more than 130 years, and like the Met, it's so huge you can't possibly see everything all at once. There are 25 buildings and 46 exhibition halls. Head to the fourth floor to see the dinosaurs. Say "hi" to the T. rex, apatosaurus, stegosaurus, and triceratops. Stop at some of the computers to find out more about these dinos. Make sure to see the dinosaur nest.

Kids also like to see the huge dioramas in the mammal halls on the first, second, and third floors that show you the animals in their native habitats—they've got Alaskan brown bear, African elephants, water buffaloes from Asia, plus many others!

Don't miss the giant totem poles in the Hall of Northwest Coast Indians on the first floor, the museum's oldest hall. It opened in 1896!

You'll probably also want to see the giant 94-foot model of a blue whale. She weighs 21,000 pounds! You can find it on the first floor in the Milstein Hall of Ocean Life, and when you get there, you'll be staring at the biggest model of the biggest creature that ever lived on earth.

For ocean lovers, there are lots of other dioramas—of sea lions, dolphins, flying fish, and more. You can find hands-on activities about the living oceans in the Kids and Families section of the museum website, www.amnh.org.

If you like rocks, you'll love the Arthur Ross Hall of Meteorites, the Morgan Memorial Hall of Gems, and the

{ What's Cool? The mummies in the Metropolitan Museum of Art.

Harry Frank Guggenheim Hall of Minerals. There are more than 100,000 rocks here. Make sure to stop and look at the Star of India. It's the world's biggest blue star sapphire. The topaz crystal from Brazil weighs 596 pounds. Check out the Cape York meteorite. It weighs 34 tons!

The Hayden Planetarium at the museum is really cool too. You'll feel like you're in a spaceship at the Space Theater! It's all part of the big seven-floor Rose Center for Earth and Space. Follow the Cosmic Pathway through 13 billion years; don't miss the chance to see the latest news from space and rock samples and models from around the world.

The museum's Hall of Biodiversity is the place to go to see why we should all care about the environment and how to protect all different kinds of life. This is where you can visit a diorama of a rain forest from Central Africa. It stretches for 90 feet, and you can step inside to see what happens to a rain forest when people don't take care of it. See all the leaves? There are more than 500,000 here, each made by hand! How about all the bugs?

If you're visiting around the holidays, you'll love the Origami Holiday Tree decorated with fanciful Japanese origami ornaments.

Make sure to allow plenty of time for the museum's Discovery Room on the first floor. Kids and their parents

{ **What's Cool?** The Dinosaur Hall at the American Museum of Natural History is one of the largest collections in the world!

can get up close and personal with specimens, make their own exhibits, be part of a dinosaur "dig," solve puzzles, and even take apart and put together a big fossil.

Check off what you saw at the American Museum of Natural History:

- ❏ T. rex
- ❏ A brown bear
- ❏ A Native American canoe
- ❏ A totem pole
- ❏ The Cape York meteorite, the largest meteorite in the world
- ❏ A rain forest
- ❏ A giant squid
- ❏ The blue whale, the world's largest animal
- ❏ A butterfly
- ❏ The planets of our solar system
- ❏ The Hayden Sphere
- ❏ A gem
- ❏ An elephant seal

Doughnut or snail? A lot of people thought the **Guggenheim Museum** (1071 Fifth Ave.; 212-355-4965; www.guggenheim.org) was a weird building when it was built. Some people thought it looked like a snail, others a doughnut. The building was designed as a spiral by famed architect Frank Lloyd Wright, with the art hung on the walls alongside a ramp. You may think some of these paintings are weird. Take the elevator to the top and look at the art as you head down the ramp.

The Cloisters (Fort Tryon Park at 193rd Street; 212-923-3700; www.metmuseum.org/visit/visit-the-cloisters) was put together from parts of buildings that date back to the 15th century! They were brought from Europe. Kids like to come to this branch of the Metropolitan Museum overlooking the Hudson River because they can play in

DID YOU KNOW?

The **Brooklyn Children's Museum** (145 Brooklyn Ave., Brooklyn, NY; 718-735-4400; www.brooklynkids.org) was the first museum created just for kids. That was in 1899, and since then, hundreds of children's museums have opened around the world. There is also a **Children's Museum of Manhattan** (212 W. 83rd St.; 212-721-1223; www.cmom.org).

the gardens and check out the brave knights and ferocious dragons on view. Don't miss the seven gigantic Unicorn Tapestries that were woven around 1500. How many plants can you count? There are images of more than 100.

The Museum of Modern Art (11 W. 53rd St.; 212-708-9400; www.moma.org) is a great place to see some masterpieces you've seen in school like Van Gogh's *The Starry Night*, Picasso's *Les Demoiselles d'Avignon*, and Rodin's great sculpture. Check out all the exhibits of appliances and even sports cars as well as the Sculpture Garden.

Love history? Check out the **Museum of the City of New York** (1220 Fifth Ave.; 212-534-1672; www.mcny .org) where you'll especially like the exhibit of toys and dolls owned by NYC kids. And you'll also like the National **Museum of the American Indian** which represents the Smithsonian with more than 10,000 years of Native heritage (1 Bowling Green; 212-514-3700; www.nmai.si.edu).

Kid-Friendly Museum Events

There are some 150 museums in New York City, and many have free evenings and special activities for kids and families. Check museum websites before you go to see if there are any special exhibits you want to catch. Here are the websites for some of the museums kids most like to visit in NYC. You can find links to others at www.nycgo.com/.

American Folk Art Museum: Columbus Ave. at 66th St.; (212) 595-9533; www.folkartmuseum.org.

American Museum of Natural History: Central Park West at 79th St.; (212) 769-5100; www.amnh.org.

Brooklyn Children's Museum: 145 Brooklyn Ave., Brooklyn; (718) 735-4400; www.brooklynkids.org.

Brooklyn Museum: 200 Eastern Parkway, Brooklyn; (718) 638-5000; www.brooklynmuseum.org.

Children's Museum of Manhattan: 212 W. 83rd St.; (212) 721-1223; www.cmom.org.

El Museo del Barrio about Latino culture: 1230 Fifth Ave.; (212) 831-7272; www.elmuseo.org.

Guggenheim Museum: 1071 Fifth Ave.; (212) 423-3500; www.guggenheim.org.

Intrepid Sea, Air & Space Museum: Pier 86, W. 46th St. and 12th Ave.; (212) 245-0072; www.intrepidmuseum.org.

Lower East Side Tenement Museum: 103 Orchard St.; (212) 982-8420; www.tenement.org.

Metropolitan Museum of Art: 1000 Fifth Ave.; (212) 535-7710; www.metmuseum.org.

Museum of Arts and Design: 2 Columbus Circle; (212) 299-7777; www.madmuseum.org.

Museum of Modern Art: 11 W. 53rd St.; (212) 708-9400; www.moma.org.

The Paley Center for Media: 25 W. 52nd St.; (212) 621-6600; www.paleycenter.org.

Museum of the City of New York: 1220 Fifth Ave.; (212) 534-1672; www.mcny.org.

Museum of the Moving Image in Queens: 36-01 35th Ave.; (718) 777-6888; www.movingimage.us.

National Museum of the American Indian: Alexander Hamilton U.S. Custom House, One Bowling Green; (212) 514-3700; www.nmai.si.edu.

New Museum: 235 Bowery; (212) 219-1222; www.new museum.org.

NYC's Jewish Museum: 1109 Fifth Ave. (at 92nd St.); (212) 423-3200; www.jewishmuseum.org.

TELL THE ADULTS:

- Don't go into a museum when you're tired and hungry.

- Wear comfortable shoes.

- Look on the museum website or ask when you arrive to see if there are special family activities that day or if there's a special area of the museum just for kids. If you're lucky, you'll also get to meet some NYC kids.

- Because some museums are too big to see in a few hours, zero in on a few exhibits you want to see. Don't worry about not seeing everything.

- Get some postcards at the gift shop when you arrive and have a scavenger hunt to see how many "treasures" you can find.

- Leave time at the end for the gift shop. Museums usually have cool stuff for kids, and in some cases, they have special kids' shops.

- See if you can take one of the Museum Highlights Tours that are offered several times a day at the Metropolitan Museum of Art. And don't forget to pick up some special family guides from the information desk.

- The Roof Garden overlooking Central Park in the Metropolitan Museum of Art is a good place to take a break—and see giant sculptures that change every year.

DID YOU KNOW?

The **American Museum of Natural History** has more than 32 million objects and specimens. The Metropolitan Museum of Art has more than 2 million objects in its collections. But not everything is on view at once. Both museums are on every family's top to-do list when they visit NYC. That's why there are more visitors from out of town here than New Yorkers. More people visit the two museums than live in most American cities!

The largest framed painting in the **Metropolitan Museum of Art** is *Washington Crossing the Delaware* by Emanuel Leutze. It was painted in 1851 and is 12 feet, 5 inches high and 21 feet, 3 inches wide. You can find it in the Peter Jay Sharp Foundation Gallery of the newly renovated American Wing.

4
PLAY BALL!

Anywhere you go in the city,

you're bound to see someone wearing a Yankees or Mets hat, a Knicks T-shirt, or maybe a Jets or Giants jersey.

New York City is home to millions of dedicated fans, whether the teams win or lose. There is also the chance to watch special sporting events such as college basketball tournaments, track and field championships, professional ice-skating, and even dog shows!

If you want to see a New York sporting event, **Madison Square Garden** (www.thegarden.com) is a great place to go. Located on Seventh Avenue between 31st and 32nd Streets, Madison Square Garden is the home of the New York Knicks basketball team (www.nba.com/knicks), **New York Rangers** hockey team (http://rangers.nhl.com), and the professional women's basketball team, **The New York Liberty** (www.wnba.com/liberty). The **New Jersey Nets** basketball team (www.nba.com/nets) plays across the Hudson River in New Jersey.

Love tennis? Come in late August and early September for the **US Open Tennis Championship** (www.usopen.org) in Flushing Meadows. The **Nassau Veterans Memorial Coliseum** out in Uniondale, Long Island, is home to the professional

A NYC KID SAYS:
"You get a great view if you sit at the seats at the top of Yankee Stadium!"
—Francesca, 9, NYC

hockey team the **New York Islanders** (http://islanders .nhl.com), or you can head to New Jersey to see the **New Jersey Devils** (http://devils.nhl.com) play hockey at the Prudential Center.

Also, the MetLife Stadium in East Rutherford, New Jersey is where two famous New York football teams, the **New York Giants** (www.giants.com) and the **New York Jets** (www.newyorkjets.com), play.

New York City has two great baseball stadiums, which are home to two great ball clubs. There is Citi Field in Flushing, Queens, where the **New York Mets** play (http:// newyork.mets.mlb.com) and Yankee Stadium, home to those Bronx Bombers, the **New York Yankees** (http:// newyork.yankees.mlb.com).

If you go to a Mets or Yankees game, you have to try a stadium hot dog or ice cream. Who knows, maybe you'll catch a fly ball out in the stands! And, your face may even be put up on the big screen TV where everyone can see you! If you want this to happen, it's helpful to wear plenty of team gear and show some spirit!

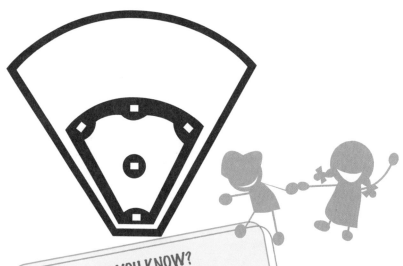

DID YOU KNOW?

More than two million New Yorkers line the streets every fall to cheer on the marathoners—more than 45,000 finishers in 2010.

There is a carousel and skatepark at Pier 62 on the Hudson River (www.hudson riverpark.org), part of a 9-acre park. The skatepark has 15,000 square feet of whorls, turns, and dives.

"Go to a Yankees game definitely. It's fun. They sell soft ice cream in little baseball caps. The fans are really energetic and noisy, and the music is good. At the 7th inning, the guys who sweep the field do the YMCA dance. Knicks and Rangers games are also really fun because Madison Square Garden is exciting. You don't need expensive seats because it's easy to see everything on the big TV screens. The food is also really good."

—Regan, 11, NYC

DID YOU KNOW?

The **New York Yankees** (http://newyork.yankees .mlb.com) and **New York Mets** (http://newyork .mets.mlb.com) are playing in brand-new stadiums. So are the **Giants** (www.giants.com) and the **Jets** (www.newyorkjets.com) of the National Football League—they are sharing the new MetLife Stadium in New Jersey. All of these new stadiums were built next door to their predecessors (Yankee Stadium, Shea Stadium, and Giants Stadium, respectively), which have since been demolished.

TELL THE ADULTS:

- Finding tickets to a New York sporting event is not as hard as some may think—although it does depend on what game you want to see. If you want to get them online, www.ticketmaster.com is a very simple way to find tickets, and there are many other websites that you can try as well. Or, you can try calling or going to the box office at the arena or stadium that is holding the event you want to see. You can often buy tickets from people selling them outside the stadium—but be careful. The prices you pay outside the stadium may be unreasonably high, and you could be getting a counterfeit ticket.

- If you can't get tickets to see the Yankees or the Mets, try a minor league team like the **Brooklyn Cyclones** (www.brooklyncyclones.com) on Coney Island.

- The **Downtown Boathouse** offers free kayaking trips and instruction on the Hudson River from Pier 40 and Pier 96 (www.downtownboathouse.org).

- Ice-skating is expensive and crowded at **Rockefeller Center Ice Rink** outside Rockefeller Center, but it is really fun too (W. 49th St. and Fifth Ave.; www.rockefellercenter.com/tour-and-explore/the-ice-skating-rink/).

DID YOU KNOW?

The walkway leading into the arena at Madison Square Garden is now known as the "Walk of Fame" and recognizes performers, athletes, announcers, and coaches who have all demonstrated amazing things throughout their career, including Patrick Ewing (who played for the Knicks) and Wayne Gretzky and Mark Messier (who both played for the Rangers).

All city marathons are modeled on the **ING New York City Marathon.** Every year the NYC Marathon Team for Kids—runners from around the world—raises money on behalf of New York Road Runners youth services to help NYC kids be more active.

The Red Sox have never forgiven the Yankees for stealing Babe Ruth, so whenever the two teams play, it's considered a grudge match.

The **New York Botanical Garden** has a special Adventure Garden where kids can run around (2900 Southern Blvd., Bronx, NY; 718-817-8700; www.nybg.org).

Sports in the Park

Take your pick. You can ice-skate; in-line skate; ride horses; play tennis, basketball, or soccer; sail model boats; even play chess in Central Park (www.centralparknyc.org). And you can borrow or rent what you need to do it.

Rent in-line and roller skates at Wollman Rink on the East Side between 62nd and 63rd Streets, where you can also rent ice skates and skate in the winter.

Rent bicycles, even two-seater tandems, at the Loeb Boathouse parking lot at East 74th Street, daily from March through October.

Borrow a basketball to play at the North Meadow Recreation Center, mid park at 97th Street.

Fish at the Harlem Meer, stocked with a wide variety of fish, at the northeast corner of the park.

Rent a rowboat April through October at the Loeb Boathouse (East Side between 74th and 75th Streets) to take out on Central Park's 22-acre lake (www.thecentralpark boathouse.com).

Play chess or checkers at the special tables inside the park at 65th Street just west of the Dairy where you can borrow chess or checker pieces.

Sail your own model sailboat at Conservatory Water (East Side between 72nd and 75th Streets) or call Central Park Sailboats at (917) 796-1382.

You can also snooze under a tree, climb some rocks, chase your sister, or play Frisbee.

Chelsea Piers—Come and Play!

If you're in New York and you're looking for a great place to take part in some sports, instead of just watching them, **Chelsea Piers Sports and Entertainment Complex** (www.chelseapiers.com) is the perfect place to head! Located between 17th and 23rd Streets along the Hudson River, Chelsea Piers contains a golf club, a sports center, a sky rink (ice rink), a field house, a roller rink, and a bowling alley. If you head on over to Chelsea Piers, you can take part in about any sport you can imagine, such as baseball, basketball, bowling, dancing, golf, gymnastics, ice hockey, ice-skating, in-line skating, rock climbing, roller hockey, skateboarding and BMX, and soccer. It's definitely a great place to meet other kids just like you and have lots of fun!

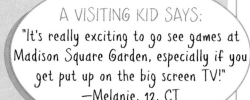

A VISITING KID SAYS:
"It's really exciting to go see games at Madison Square Garden, especially if you get put up on the big screen TV!"
—Melanie, 12, CT

5
Grab the Camera

Where can you go in the middle

of New York City and see five states? The Empire State Building, of course.

On a clear day you can see New Jersey, Connecticut, Pennsylvania, Massachusetts, as well as New York, from the Observatory on the 86th floor.

New Yorkers look forward to seeing the colored lights on the Empire State Building from far away too—Green for St. Patrick's Day; Red, White, and Blue for Independence Day; Red and Green for the Holiday Season; among others.

No wonder so many people make the **Empire State Building** (350 Fifth Ave. between 33rd and 34th Streets; www.esbny.com) one of their first must-see stops in New York. More than 100 million people have visited the top of the building. Some people even get married here.

When you ride the elevator, you're going pretty fast, up to 1,200 feet a minute! Look around the elevator. You'll probably see parents and kids from lots of different countries.

In case you're wondering, the Empire State Building does get hit by lightning, about 100 times a year. It was designed to serve as a lightning rod for the surrounding area. When lightning strikes the tip of the Empire State Building, it travels directly—and harmlessly—down a metal conduit into the ground.

Need some exercise? You can race up the 1,575 steps from the lobby to the 86th floor. Some runners have done it in just 10 minutes.

Besides being famous for being so tall, the Empire State Building is a movie star. Remember *King Kong*? Certain parts of the movie *Elf* also take place there.

Take a good look around from the Observatory. What do you see?

Another way to see all of New York's buildings is to sail around them—on a **Circle Line Tour** (Pier 83, W. 42nd St.; 212-563-3200; www .circleline42.com). Some tours around Manhattan Island take three hours and will give you plenty of opportunities to take pictures of the Statue of Liberty, the skyline, and the Brooklyn Bridge. There's a much shorter high-speed

DID YOU KNOW?

The Empire State Building was built in just one year, winning the race (with the Chrysler Building) to be the world's tallest building at the time.

trip running from May to October kids like on *The Beast* where you race by all the skyscrapers (www .nytours.us). You've got to be 40" tall to ride. Ready for some more cool buildings? Stop in at the **Chrysler Building** (405 Lexington Ave.). The old-fashioned, art deco lobby is worth a stop because there aren't many like it. When Walter Chrysler built his skyscraper in 1930, he wanted the company's headquarters to make people think about his cars. The spire on top looks like a car radiator grille. There are decorations throughout the building that look like old-fashioned hood ornaments, wheels, and cars. Don't miss all the weird gargoyles on the building. There are even transportation scenes painted on the ceiling. How many can you find?

Stop in at **Grand Central Terminal** (42nd Street at Park Ave.; www.grandcentralterminal.com) while you're nearby. It's been a landmark since 1913. Half a million commuters use this terminal every day. It's a "terminal," not a "station," because every train begins or ends its journey here. See the clock at the central information area? It's got four faces. A lot of kids like to stop in Grand Central to get a snack (head downstairs to the big food court) and then look at the blue ceiling upstairs. It's a painting of more than 2,500 stars. How many constellations can you find? Tip: little lights pinpoint them.

Quick! Think of a place in New York City where you can see your favorite music star, hear a gigantic dinosaur roar, or catch the latest news.

Stumped? Head directly to **Times Square.** At 42nd Street and Broadway, this is one of the easiest places in New York to reach by public transport since so many bus and subway lines stop here.

New York City kids like to come here because there's so much to do and see in just a few blocks. When your parents were kids, this part of town was so run down that families didn't like to walk around here much. The city has worked hard to clean up

DID YOU KNOW?

The Radio City Rockettes have been kicking up their heels in their world-famous chorus lines at **Radio City Music Hall** for more than 70 years (1260 Avenue of the Americas; www .radiocity.com). Since they started, more than 3,000 women have been Rockettes. The women all look like they're the same height, but it's an illusion. The tallest women are at the center with the shortest at either end. Besides performing in the Radio City Christmas spectacular, the Rockettes perform at the tree lighting ceremony at Rockefeller Center, during Macy's Thanksgiving Day Parade, and even the presidential inauguration.

and rebuild Times Square in the last fifteen years, and now it's usually the first place kids like to come when they visit New York! A lot of people say it's like a city theme park with cool restaurants, big stores (check out **M&M's World** on Broadway near 49th St. with every color of M&Ms you can imagine!), theaters, and even the world's largest TV screen. There are 12,500 hotel rooms here—one-fifth of all the rooms in the city—and more than 250 restaurants.

Check out all the giant signs! Some are huge advertisements, but you can also read the latest news lit up on a moving stripe at One Times Square. Since the late nineteenth century, this has been the center of the country's theater world. And you can buy souvenirs from the street vendors or in one of the dozens of stores that line the streets.

Check out **Madame Tussaud's New York Wax Museum** (234 West 42nd St; 866-841-3505; www.nycwax.com),

A VISITING KID SAYS:
"You see pictures of the Empire State Building and all of these other places, but when you see the real thing, it's cool! Bring binoculars to the Empire State Building!"
—Scott, 11, Scottsdale, AZ

Times Square Scavenger Hunt: Can you find these things on your visit to Times Square?

- ❏ Indoor Ferris wheel

- ❏ Hot pretzel

- ❏ Booth selling Broadway tickets

- ❏ A tourist with a camera

- ❏ The theater where *The Lion King* is playing

- ❏ The latest news flash

- ❏ An "I ♥ NY" T-shirt

where you can "meet" The Hulk, Jennifer Lopez, or Michael Jordan—along with nearly 200 of their friends. Just one thing—they're all made of wax. It's not easy to pose for a wax portrait. Madame Tussaud's sculptors have to take lots of pictures and more than 250 measurements of each body. The sculptor models a clay portrait, and then the clay is molded in plaster. From that mold, the body is cast in fiberglass and the head from wax. Each pair of eyes is made individually—with hand-painted eyeballs to match the real ones. Hair color is perfectly matched to a sample given by the celebrity and each strand is inserted one by one. The same goes with teeth. It takes five weeks just to make a head—six months to create the portrait. And every day, two teams inspect each figure to see if they need any "help" before the museum opens. They regularly get their hair washed and their makeup touched up! The celebrities often donate their own clothes and shoes, so the portraits will look more real. Got your camera? You can pose for a picture with your favorite star. They look so authentic your friends might be fooled. Tip: If you whisper in J-Lo's ear, she blushes!

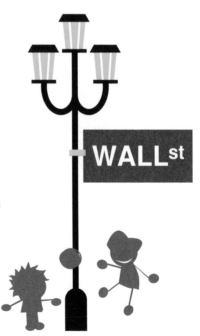

While you're on 42nd Street, peek inside **Disney's New Amsterdam Theater** (214 W. 42nd St.; http://theater.disney .go.com/faq.html) a few steps west of Times Square. It's the city's oldest Broadway theater, having opened in 1903, before a lot of your grandparents were born! And it's been completely restored. This is where *The Lion King* opened on Broadway and is still playing to huge crowds.

You can also shop till you drop at **Toys "R" Us** (Seventh Avenue and West 44th Street), the biggest Toys "R" Us anywhere. Here's where you can see the giant T. rex dinosaur, visit a three-story Barbie house, ride the indoor Ferris wheel, or try out the latest video games, ready and waiting.

You can visit all the little shops and street vendors selling "I ♥ NY" T-shirts, NYPD and NYFD hats, and replicas and key chains of the Statue of Liberty. What souvenir will you want to take home?

Lots of families like to see a play when they're in New York City. You might get to go to one of the big Broadway theaters, or even see what is called an Off Broadway play. That means it's a smaller, less glitzy production, shown someplace other than the big Broadway theaters. Tickets usually are cheaper too. Would you like to be an actor? Sometimes kids have parts in Broadway productions. They still have to go to school and do their homework, maybe in between their scenes. Sometimes they'll even move to New York City with their mom or dad temporarily to appear in a play. When they graduate from school, a lot of young people come to New York to audition for roles on Broadway. Many also work in restaurants as waiters or waitresses. Next time you're out at a restaurant, ask your server if he or she is an actor!

Make sure to eat something before you head to the theater. Otherwise, plays can seem awfully long (you can buy snacks in the theaters, but they're usually expensive).

Despite all the activities, one of the best things to do in Times Square is just watch all the people. They are speaking so many different languages. Some are wearing really crazy outfits. Watch out! It seems like everyone's in a big hurry!

Sightseeing Smarts

New York is so big, and there's so much to do! You can't see it all. Here's how to have fun sightseeing:

Wear comfortable shoes.

Look at a map or program one into your phone so you know where you're going. (You can get a map at your hotel.)

Stash some snacks and a camera in your pocket.

Alternate sites you want to see like a museum or the Empire State Building with some people-watching, time in the park, or time out for a meal. That way you won't get so tired!

When you get really tired, take a break. You can go to a playground (there are more than 200 in the city!), get something to eat, or go back to the hotel and chill.

Alternate what you want to do and what your parents want you to see. That way everybody gets to lead the pack— some of the time.

Holiday Glitter

You've probably seen it on TV. There's been a big Christmas Tree in front of **Rockefeller Center** (www.rockefellercenter .com) since 1931! A special team goes all around the East Coast looking for the perfect tree. The Rockefeller Center Tree starts in someone's backyard where it's been growing for years and years. When asked, families donate the tree, which is then carefully brought into NYC with a police escort on a custom-made trailer. It takes at least 15 people and a 280-ton crane to handle the tree. More than 26,000 light-emitting diodes and five miles of wire decorate the tree. The same star has been used on top for more than 50 years. It's 5 feet wide! Of course the tree can be 100 feet tall. After the holidays, the tree is ground into mulch and used in the city's parks.

A VISITING KID SAYS:
"In the winter, it's really fun to go ice-skating at Rockefeller Center."
—Shelby, 9, NJ

Circus!

New York kids love the circus as much as kids everywhere. If you're visiting in the fall or winter, you might want to see the **Big Apple Circus,** the one-ring circus under a Big Top tent that's become a holiday tradition for New York families (Cunningham Park, 196-22 Union Turnpike, Queens, NY; 800-922-3772; www.bigapplecircus.com). There are acrobats, jugglers, dogs, clowns, flying trapeze artists, and more.

   Ringling Brothers Barnum & Bailey Circus comes to New York City in the spring. Check www.ringling.com to see when the circus will be in town. There's also an area on the website for kids. A tip: Go early and you might be able to talk to the animals.

The United Nations

The United Nations Building (First Avenue between 42nd and 46th Streets; www.un.org) towers over the East River and is another must-see site. Your parents definitely will think so. The UN, of course, is the voluntary organization that countries around the world have joined to help keep peace, develop friendlier relations among different countries, and to help poor people live better. Maybe you've collected pennies for UNICEF at Halloween time. That is a United Nations effort. Certainly you've heard about UN peacekeeping troops being sent to different countries around the world. Take a guided tour. You'll learn a lot about the work the delegates and staff do here as well as about the building. Have you ever seen so many people from so many different countries in one building?

DID YOU KNOW?

The pair of marble lions that stands outside the **New York Public Library** at Fifth Avenue and 42nd Street has been welcoming New Yorkers since the library opened in 1911 (www.nypl.org). First they were called Leo Astor and Leo Lenox, after New York Public Library founders John Jacob Astor and James Lenox. But during the 1930s, Mayor Fiorello La Guardia dubbed them Patience and Fortitude, for the qualities he thought New Yorkers needed to survive the Great Depression. And these names have stuck. Patience is on the south side of the steps and Fortitude on the north. If you visit at holiday time, they might have giant wreaths around their necks.

6

Lady Liberty &
Ellis Island

The Statue of Liberty

(www.nps.gov/stli) was a thank-you gift from France to the US that took more than 20 years to arrive.

And when she did come, she was packed in 214 crates, like a giant jigsaw puzzle that had to be put together. Good thing they sent directions along too.

But what a present the Statue of Liberty turned out to be! Originally planned as a gift of the people of France to the people of the US to commemorate their long friendship, she stands in New York Harbor as the most famous symbol of liberty and freedom in the world. She's also the biggest metal statue ever constructed.

A NYC KID SAYS:
"There are a lot of souvenirs at the Statue of Liberty and it's a lot of fun."
—Sarah, 9, NYC

DID YOU KNOW?

The Statue of Liberty is green because it's made of copper and copper oxidizes when exposed to the air. It took 30 years for the statue to turn green!

When you're visiting the **Statue of Liberty** and **Ellis Island,** you're visiting a national park (www.nps.gov/stli).

Immigrants cried when they saw her because they knew their long sea voyage was over. Today, a lot of people get choked up when they see Lady Liberty all lit up for the first time.

To get to the Statue of Liberty, you ride a ferry (201-604-2800; www.statue cruises.com) from Battery Park across New York Harbor to Liberty Island. It takes about 15 minutes, and then you can get back on the same ferry to visit Ellis Island.

The original idea was that the French people would build the statue and transport it to the US. The Americans were supposed to build the pedestal on which she would stand. The French raised the money they needed. But in the US, no one seemed to want to give any money to help.

Finally, the *New York World*, a 19th-century newspaper, launched a big campaign to raise the needed funds. Even schoolkids contributed. People all around the country started to send money, and just before the statue arrived in 1885, enough money had been raised to build the pedestal. She was unveiled the next year, in October 1886.

The sculptor Frédéric Auguste Bartholdi used his mom as the model for the Statue of Liberty's face. He spent more than 20 years on the project and put a lot of symbols into her. For example, the seven rays of her crown are supposed to represent the seven seas and the seven continents. The tablet she holds is engraved with the date of American independence, July IV, MDCCLXXVI (July 4, 1776), and her torch means she's lighting the way to freedom and liberty. At her feet are chains to symbolize her escaping the chains of tyranny.

On the second floor of the Statue Pedestal, you can see replicas of the statue's face and foot. They are big! And just think of the work it took to create this colossal statue.

She's made of copper sheets with an iron framework. It wasn't easy. The framework was designed and built by Gustave Eiffel, the great French engineer who later built the Eiffel Tower.

ELLIS ISLAND

Ellis Island is north of Liberty Island, about a 10- to 15-minute ferry ride on the Circle Line-Statue of Liberty Ferry from Battery Park. Maybe someone in your family arrived in the US here. Before 1892, individual states oversaw immigration, but as the numbers of immigrants increased, it got to be too big of a job.

A NYC KID SAYS:
"Going on the boat to Ellis Island and the Statue of Liberty is really fun."
—Richard, 9, NYC

The Great Hall, where the immigrants waited when they arrived on Ellis Island, is part of the museum. Look around. Do you think you would have been scared, not speaking the language, wearing clothes that looked different? Probably you would have been hungry and possibly sick after two weeks on a rocking boat.

Between 1892 and 1954, 12 million immigrants passed through Ellis Island. Each one had to pass a six-second medical exam in the Great Hall before they could enter the US to see if they had any of 60 different diseases like diphtheria, measles, or any other contagious illness or disability that would keep them from being able to earn a living. Ninety-eight percent passed.

It's important to remember that everyone who came to the US in those days didn't have to come through Ellis

DID YOU KNOW?

People in New York City come from 188 different countries and nearly half speak a second language at home.

You can also walk on the pedestrian walkway of the Brooklyn Bridge—the biggest suspension bridge in the world when it was built. Bring your camera. The views of New York City are great.

Island—not if they had more money. "Steerage," or third-class, passengers were the ones who landed here after upward of two weeks on crowded ships where they

faced rough seas without much chance to get any fresh air.

When you visit Ellis Island, you can watch a movie about the immigrants who came here. Sometimes, professional actors bring to life the stories that immigrants have told over the years. Check when you arrive to see what time these plays start.

You might also get to see the reenactment of an immigrant hearing, just as it would have been conducted to determine whether the immigrant could stay in the US.

You'll get to visit the Treasures from Home Collection and see what the immigrants brought with them. How

many toys and dolls do you see? You'll see the baggage room where thousands of immigrants checked their bags while they waited to be "inspected."

If you come from a family of immigrants, you might want to take the chance to learn how to trace your family roots or look up a relative on the huge electronic database at the American Family Immigration History Center. There are ships' passenger records of more than 22 million people from 1892 to 1924, when immigration processing was at its peak at Ellis Island. If you find your relative's name, you can get reproductions of the original lists of passengers and photos of the ships.

Make sure to stop at the American Immigrant Wall of Honor, just outside the "peopling of America" exhibit. The wall is inscribed with more than 600,000 names of those who came through Ellis Island. Families have paid to have their immigrant relative's names engraved.

You can really understand looking at all those different names from all those different countries and cultures why people call this country a melting pot. Your own family probably is one too. How many different countries do your relatives come from?

A lot of kids who come to NYC try food they haven't eaten at home. Check off what you've tried:

❑ a hot dog from a street vendor

❑ a hot salted pretzel or roasted nuts from a street vendor

❑ a slice of NYC pizza folded in half (that's the way New Yorkers eat it)

❑ a pastrami sandwich

❑ a fresh bagel with a shmear (of cream cheese)

❑ Chinatown noodles or rice with chopsticks

{ What's Cool? Trying a kind of food you've never tasted.

Grab a tape measure!

The height from the foot of the Statue of Liberty to the tip of the flame is 151 feet, one inch (from the ground, 305 feet, one inch). She weighs 225 tons (445,000 pounds).
She's one big lady!

Her index finger: 8 feet

Her head: 17 feet, 3 inches

Nose: 4 feet

Right arm: 42 feet

Mouth: 3 feet wide (when she's not smiling)

DID YOU KNOW?

It's 354 steps from the entrance to the crown of the Statue of Liberty.

You get a terrific view of the Statue of Liberty on the free Staten Island Ferry across New York Harbor.

You've probably heard some of these words: "Give me your tired, your poor, your huddled masses yearning to breathe free." They're part of a very famous poem written in 1883 by Emma Lazarus. You can read the entire poem on a plaque in the statue museum.

Becoming a Citizen

The US is often called a melting pot or salad bowl because so many immigrants have come here from different countries and cultures looking for a better life. Many children whose parents are immigrants are citizens because they were born here. But just living here doesn't automatically make you a citizen. If you've come to the US from another country, to become a citizen you must:

–Be at least 18.

–Live in the US for five years or more.

–Be of good moral character and loyal to the US.

–Be able to read, write, and speak basic English to pass a test.

–Have enough basic knowledge of the US government and history to pass a test.

–Be willing to take an oath of allegiance to the US.

Once you've filed all the necessary documents and passed the tests, you appear before a judge and ask to become a citizen. You take a special oath. It's a very exciting day. Many immigrants live in the US their whole lives without becoming citizens.

South Street Seaport

Welcome to the "Street of Ships!" You can travel back in time at South Street Seaport around Pier 17 on the East River (www.southstreetseaport.com). For more than 300 years, the seaport was one of the city's commercial centers, handling all of the goods that were coming in and out of the port by ship—China clippers, Atlantic packets, Caribbean schooners, grain barges from the Midwest. But by the mid 20th century, the port's activity had moved elsewhere in the city. Almost a century passed before the city focused on South Street Seaport again. It has been redeveloped as a place to shop, eat, and learn a little history at the **South Street Seaport Museum** (17 Fulton St.; 212-748-8600; www.seany.org). Go on board one of the ships. Check and see if there's a special family activity for parents and kids. They have a lot of them on weekends.

A NYC KID SAYS:
"South Street Seaport is cool because you get to go on the old boats."
—Jesse, 10, NYC

Pack Your Trunk!

When immigrants came in the last century, there was no e-mail, no TV, no Facebook, and most people didn't have telephones. The only way to find out more about life in America was by writing a letter to a relative already here. Sometimes, they exchanged photos so they'd know whom to look for when they arrived. Some teenagers came by themselves. If you were coming to America, you could only bring one small trunk with 30 things. You can see some of what immigrants chose to bring with them in the Treasures from Home exhibit on the third floor of the museum on Ellis Island. What would you bring?

{ **What's Cool?** Walking around the Lower East Side and seeing what bargains you can find from the street peddlers.

7

Eggrolls, Pizza,
Giant Balloons &
Bargains

Grab your chopsticks!

Everyone who comes to New York for the first time should have dinner in Chinatown. With the Chinese lanterns and telephone booths, everyone speaking Chinese, it's like stepping into a Chinese city right in downtown New York. There are hundreds of restaurants to choose from.

You'll hear more Chinese spoken than English here in Lower Manhattan just south of Canal Street and a short walk from the Lower East Side. Even the street signs are in Chinese.

Browse in stores along Mott Street that sell Chinese toys, herbs, and all kinds of strange-looking foods. If you want to

A NYC KID SAYS:

"I love eating in Chinatown. Try the pork or the crab, and if you pay attention, you can even learn how to use chopsticks!"
—Laurel, 11, Queens, NY

DID YOU KNOW?

Bloomingdale's (1000 Third Ave. at 59th Street; 212-705-2000; www.bloomingdales.com) was started in the late 1800s on the Lower East Side by two brothers, Joseph and Lyman Bloomingdale, selling hoop skirts. They moved uptown to Lexington Avenue and 59th Street in 1886.

A NYC KID SAYS:

"Bloomingdale's is a big store with a lot of different things. It's fun to just look around. If you visit and don't know where to find something, just ask someone who works here. The store is very organized."
—Sarah, 11, NYC

{ What's Cool? Counting how many different subway cars and buses you've been on while in NYC. There are 6,356 subway cars in New York City and 4,372 buses to choose from.

learn more about the history of Chinatown and the people who settled here, stop in at the **Museum of Chinese in America** (215 Centre St.; 212-619-4785; www.mocanyc.org).

Of course you're going to eat. The restaurants here are big—and tiny. Sometimes, the waiters don't speak English, but the menus often are printed in Chinese and English. Any kind of noodle dish is a good bet, New York kids say. They also like to come here on weekends for the Chinese brunch called dim sum. You pick all kinds of little dumplings from carts the waiters roll around the restaurant.

Little Italy is another old-fashioned neighborhood that's a

A VISITING KID SAYS:
"Save some of your money because in New York you always find something else you want."
—Katie, 14, Philadelphia, PA

DID YOU KNOW?

FAO Schwarz, the giant toy store on Fifth Avenue and 58th Street (212-644-9400; www.fao.com) was started more than 130 years ago by four brothers who brought toys from Europe to American children—stuffed animals, dollhouses, tricycles, and sleds. A lot of the toys in those days couldn't be found elsewhere.

favorite with kids and parents. It's just north of Canal Street and Chinatown. You'll find lots of little restaurants here too where you can have pizza, pasta, lasagna, and yummy Italian pastries and ice cream. Try **Ferrara's,** which is the very first espresso bar in the country and serves yummy gelato. Some families like to go to Chinatown and Little Italy for dessert. If you're visiting in September, all of Mulberry Street becomes a huge outdoor restaurant at the Festival of San Gennaro.

Of course you can get any kind of food you want in New York from an omelet in Greenwich Village to burgers in Midtown. You will find BBQ (try Virgil's near Times Square), pizza (kids like John's Pizzeria), soul food in Harlem, hot dogs from street carts, and the fanciest food

you've ever seen. Some of the country's most famous chefs live and work here. You might have fun scouting out a restaurant in Greenwich Village or SoHo where there are so many. Try the frozen hot chocolate at Serendipity 3 on the Upper East Side. Stop in at **Dylan's Candy Bar** for chocolates to bring home and share with your friends.

Girls like **American Girl Place** (609 Fifth Ave. at 49th St.; 877-247-5223; www.americangirl.com), where they come to buy dolls and doll clothes and books. It's fun to stay for tea or lunch at the cafe because their dolls get VIP treatment too and are served

{ What's Cool? Eating a piping hot pretzel from a street vendor.

on special tiny china while sitting on doll-size seats. And everyone likes the loud, funky **Ruby Foo's** (1626 Broadway at 49th St., 212-489-5600; www.rubyfoos.com).

Macy's Herald Square is still the world's biggest department store with 10 floors.

Kids think these stores are fun because they're like being in a giant treasure chest. Girls can try on makeup and perfume; boys can sample food. Everyone

can check out the latest electronics at the **Sony Wonder Technology Lab** (550 Madison Ave.; 212-833-8100; www.sonywondertechlab.com) or basketball gear at the NBA Store (590 Fifth Ave.; www.nba.com/nycstore/).

There's lots of special NYC gear too.

There are lots of other stores in NYC too—big ones and small ones. Even museums have great stores in New York. It's fun just to window-shop—and people-watch everywhere.

Don't forget your birthday money.

TELL THE ADULTS:

- There is a **New York Transit Museum** in Brooklyn (130 Livingston St.) that is the largest museum in the country devoted to urban public transportation history and offers special family programs. It also has an annex in Grand Central Terminal. You can learn more about NYC's subway stations by downloading a podcast tour at www.transit museumeducation.org/museumcast/.

> A NYC KID SAYS:
> "Take the subway when you're in a hurry. They're the quickest and buses are slower."
> —Sarah, 9, NYC

- A lot of NYC kids like to go watch the balloons getting inflated the night before the Macy's Thanksgiving Day Parade. The balloons are rolled out and anchored with sandbags to keep them from flying away. (Hint: Go to West 77th and 81st Streets between Columbus and Central Park West between 3 and 10 p.m.) The balloon lineup takes up two full city blocks!

Macy's Thanksgiving Day Parade

Camels and elephants were part of the first Macy's Parade held on Thanksgiving Day 1924. Horses pulled the floats!

Today of course, the entire world watches the parade on TV, and millions of parents and kids line the route in New York City. There are bands—they compete from all over the country to get a spot—clowns, floats, singers, dancers including the Radio City Rockettes, and of course, the giant balloons.

The balloons have been a Macy's Parade tradition since 1927. In fact, to blow up the giant balloons Macy's uses more helium than anyone else in the country except the US government. A team of 10 artists works on designing and building the balloons all year long.

A NYC KID SAYS:
"If you go to the Macy's Thanksgiving Parade, wear a lot of layers. It gets freezing!"
—Ronni, 9, NYC

Calling All Bargain Lovers

Every Sunday Orchard Street is closed to traffic from Delancey Street to E. Houston Street so merchants can put their merchandise out onto the street like in the old days. (Remember, Houston Street is pronounced, "HOW-ston street" by New Yorkers.)

More than 100 years ago, when immigrant families lived in the tall tenements in Lower Manhattan, peddlers hit the streets selling their wares out of potato sacks. They expanded to pushcarts and eventually storefronts selling everything from pots and pans to underwear to vegetables. The website for the Lower East Side area of stores and restaurants is www.lowereastsideny.com.

New Yorkers have always come to Orchard Street and the surrounding neighborhood looking for bargains. Today, they also come for cutting-edge fashion and great food, like dill pickles, deli sandwiches, knishes, and more. Stop in at **Katz's Delicatessen,** the city's oldest (205 E. Houston St.; 212-254-2246; http://katzsdelicatessen.com). It's been dishing out pastrami sandwiches since 1888!

You'll still find great bargains on everything from leather jackets to purses to jewelry, perfume, and shoes. Don't be afraid to bargain: The storeowners expect it! Stop in at the **Lower East Side Tenement Museum** (108 Orchard St.; 212-982-8420; www.tenement.org).

A VISITING KID SAYS:
"I love Chinatown and the Lower East Side for the knock-off Gucci purses and Tiffany jewelry, and it's really fun to bargain and get what you want for less money."
—Colleen, 13, Long Island, NY

8

Horns, Drums,
Songs & More!

Anywhere you go in the city, you are bound to find it:

Music is always in the air. It's in the parks, in the giant concert halls, on the street corners, and even down in the subway stations! You can hear anything from classical music, to opera, jazz, some pop, and more. It all really depends on where you head.

A NYC KID SAYS:

"The best part about Central Park is all the cool shows they have there in the summer. This summer I went to see Dave Matthews, but it was too crowded. I think Lenny Kravitz played there a while back. And sometimes my parents take me to those operas on the big lawn. Those are cool because all my friends are there too."
—Kelly, 14, Manhattan

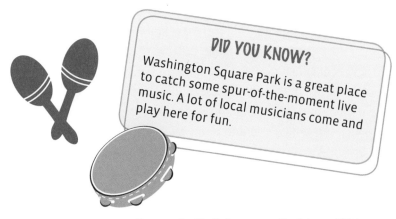

DID YOU KNOW?

Washington Square Park is a great place to catch some spur-of-the-moment live music. A lot of local musicians come and play here for fun.

If you go over to **Carnegie Hall** (you can find it on 57th Street and Seventh Avenue), you can hear classical, jazz, and other types of music by famous groups from around the world. There are a lot of family concerts too. As you walk inside, you will be entering a concert hall so beautiful that it is actually a National Historic Landmark!

Do you like hearing big orchestras with lots of instruments or watching dancers twirl across the stage? At **Lincoln Center** (www.lincolncenter.org) on the Upper West Side between 62nd and 65th Streets, you can find plenty of symphonies and ballets performed by really amazing musicians and dancers. Want to join in and play some music of your own? Chamber Music Society of Lincoln Center has a "Meet the Music!" series for kids and their families, where you can

A VISITING KID SAYS:

"Seeing a concert in NYC was pretty amazing because everyone was so happy just to be there and to be listening to the music. It felt really personal because we were able to get really close to the stage."
—Amanda, 16, CT

take a musical journey into the world of chamber music, a type of music performed by a small group of musicians (www.chambermusicsociety.org).

Have you ever seen the *Nutcracker* performed live on stage? In New York, the *Nutcracker* is a holiday tradition at the Lincoln Center. You can see the ballet suite around Christmas time every year, and kids from all over the city take part in it! Can you imagine playing a mouse, Arabian, or candy cane on a stage at the Lincoln Center?

The **Brooklyn Academy of Music** (www.bam.org) has lots of family workshops and concerts too.

Have you ever seen an opera? The **Metropolitan Opera** (www.metopera.org) has special kid-friendly performances of pieces like *Hansel and Gretel* and Mozart's *Magic Flute* at Lincoln Center.

If you love dance, you have plenty of options, too, from **American Ballet Theatre** (www.abt.org) to the **New York City Ballet** (www.nycballet.com) to the **Alvin Ailey American Dance Theater** (www.alvinailey.org), plus much more.

Do you like being outside and listening to music? Central Park offers many concerts throughout the summer, and most of them are free. You can see shows ranging from some of your parents' favorite older artists to some of your favorite pop performers! So if you are going to be traveling to NYC in the summertime, you should check to see who is going to be playing in the park when you are there (www.centralpark.com/guide/activities/concerts.html). Maybe it will be someone you would like to see!

Finally, if you head on down to the South Street Seaport around Pier 17 on the East River, you can hear sea chanteys, country and western music, bluegrass, and jazz. You can find plenty of festivals there, and plenty of musicians playing out on the street corners.

So wherever you go, music is definitely in the air. And these are absolutely some of the best places to find it. Get out there and enjoy!

TELL THE ADULTS:

- The NYC orchestras, operas, and dance companies often offer public rehearsals and special programs for families. Check their websites to see what will be offered when you visit. A good place to start your search is www.nycgo.com.

A NYC KID SAYS:
"Ballet isn't just for girls. It's a lot of fun to watch. You should go see it."
—Wells, 10, NYC

9

Monkeys, Elephants, Polar Bears & Alice in Wonderland

Let's have some fun in the sun ...

or the snow. It doesn't matter. Central Park is the place New York kids go to play, and you can too.

There's plenty of room for sure. Central Park stretches for 50 city blocks between the Upper East and West Sides—843 acres smack in the middle of Manhattan.

It's been here for 150 years, since the city paid for a chunk of land that back then was virtually a dump. Today some New Yorkers pay just as much as the city did then for apartments just to overlook the park.

Maybe you'll want to take a horse-drawn carriage ride through the park. You'll see them lining up just outside the park on 59th Street, at the south end of the park.

When you get to the park, stop in at **The Dairy** at the south end of the park. In the 1870s, city children could get fresh milk here. Now the Victorian building is the Park Visitor Center and Gift

> **A NYC KID SAYS:**
> "You should definitely go to the merry-go-round and skate on Wollman Rink at night and go to the zoo— the polar bears are really cool."
> —Chris, 10, NYC

Shop where you can pick up a map and find out what's happening in the park the day you're there.

Nearby, you'll find the **Wollman Rink** (www.wollman skatingrink.com), where a lot of kids like to ice-skate in the winter, and in the summer the rink is transformed into a little amusement park called **Victorian Gardens** (to get there enter Central Park from 59th Street and Sixth Avenue and walk north; 212-982-2229; www.victoriangardensnyc.com).

Then check out the **Central Park Zoo** (at 64th Street and Fifth Avenue; www.centralparkzoo.com). You might get to see the polar bears tear open their Christmas presents.

DID YOU KNOW?

There are 21 different playgrounds in **Central Park** and more than 200 across the city. The websites www.centralparknyc.org and www.nycgovparks.org can steer you to all the city play lots.

Central Park is a great place to meet local kids.

You'll love the penguins, polar bears, sea lions, monkeys, and more. There's even a roaring waterfall and tropical birds.

There's a great playground near the Children's Zoo complete with a 45-foot spiral slide. Don't miss the George Delacorte Musical Clock. It's right near the Children's Zoo, and every hour a nursery rhyme plays while a bear with a tambourine, a hippo with a violin, a goat with panpipes, a kangaroo with horns, and a penguin with a drum glide around the base.

In the middle of the park at West 72nd Street, heading north, you'll pass Strawberry Fields. This is one of the park's most visited spots and was named to honor John Lennon, who lived nearby and could see this spot from his apartment building. It's an international peace garden with plants from every country in the world. Look for the mosaic in the pathway. It's inscribed with IMAGINE to remind people of the message of peace in Lennon's song.

A NYC KID SAYS:
"Go biking in Central Park."
—Liam, 8, NYC

A lot of kids also like to hang out in the **Sheep Meadow.** (Yes, there were sheep here in the park's first years.)

Cross a bridge yet? There are 36 bridges in the park—no two of them

A VISITING KID SAYS:

"My favorite memory of New York was going there with my grandparents and cousin and riding on the horse-drawn carriage through Central Park."
—Rachel, 10, Boston, MA

DID YOU KNOW?

There are over 9,000 benches in Central Park. They would stretch 7 miles if placed end to end.

There are 24,000 trees and 250 acres of lawn in Central Park—plenty of places to run around!

alike—and 58 miles of paths where you can walk, run, or ride horses and bikes.

The old-fashioned carousel is in the middle of the park at 64th Street. It's one of the biggest in the whole country!

Keep an eye out for **Alice in Wonderland.** You'll find her along with the Cheshire Cat, the Mad Hatter, and the Dormouse at the northern end of the Conservatory Water where kids and grown-ups like to sail model boats.

Try sliding down her toadstool seat! Kids also like the Hans Christian Andersen statue showing him reading

"The Ugly Duckling." Kids like to climb onto the book—and the duck.

Say hi to **Balto the Dog** (at East 67th Street near the East Drive). Balto was the leader of the husky sled team that carried the serum across Alaska to save people from dying of diphtheria. Bet you didn't think you were going to learn a little history here in the park!

Of course, you'd probably prefer to run around, climb some rocks, or have a picnic under a tree. Where's the Frisbee?

While you're in the park, see if you can find these special things . . .

❏ Balto the sled dog

❏ Alice in Wonderland

❏ Mother Goose

❏ The carousel

❏ The Dairy

❏ A fancy fountain

❏ A police officer on a horse

❏ Strawberry Fields

❏ A bridge

❏ A polar bear

TELL THE ADULTS:

- Enough museums! There are other fun things to do in NYC, like the activities listed below.
- The Bronx Zoo (www.bronxzoo.com) is the largest metropolitan zoo in the country. More than 4,000 animals live here, and it's well worth the trek to the Bronx.
- Central Park is a great place to take a break from museum-going, especially if you've been at the Metropolitan Museum of Art on the East Side or the American Museum of Natural History on the West Side, both of which are very close to the park. When the weather is warm enough, buy some sandwiches and have a picnic in the park.
- If it's summer, there might be a concert at Naumburg Bandshell or on the Great Lawn. They do rock concerts, operas, and classical music here. The New York Philharmonic plays here. There are also puppet shows at the Swedish Cottage Marionette Theatre at West 79th Street.
- Central Park has its own website, www.central parknyc.org, where you can take a kids' tour of the park and find out more about family programs.
- You can find information on all New York City parks and recreation at www.nycgovparks.org.
- The Central Park Zoo website is www.centralpark zoo.com.

Talk to the Animals

Take your pick. You can head to the African rain forest and visit more than 20 gorillas in the Congo Gorilla Forest. Maybe you'd rather meet Siberian tigers at Tiger Mountain. In the summer, you can wander amid 1,000 different kinds of butterflies and moths. Check out a black leopard in JungleWorld, an endangered snow leopard in the Himalayan habitat, or see all the little rodents in the Mousehouse. Take the Bengali Express Monorail through Wild Asia, past tigers, elephants, rhinos, antelopes, and more.

Get ready to roll. There's a lot of ground to cover at the **Bronx Zoo** (2300 Southern Blvd. in the Bronx; 718-220-5103; www.bronxzoo.com), and you won't want to miss anything. There is a Zoo Shuttle you can take from one part of the zoo to another and a Skyfari gondola that gets you from Asia to the Children's Zoo in no time.

At the Children's Zoo, open April through

DID YOU KNOW?

More than 200 movies have included scenes in Central Park. Have you seen Men in Black II, Stuart Little, You've Got Mail, or The Muppets Take Manhattan? Can you name another one?

October, kids can climb into child-size heron nests, walk through a prairie dog tunnel, or climb a 20-foot spiderweb made of rope. In the forest, climb up the platform 14 feet high to get face-to-face with a porcupine or look through a telescope. Remember to stop and feed the goats.

For more than 100 years, this zoo has been welcoming kids and parents. It's also a center for conservation. Hundreds of baby animals are born here every year, and zoo scientists travel around the world doing research to help protect endangered animals and environments.

Besides seeing the animals, here's your chance to learn about how you can help them survive.

A VISITING KID SAYS:
"Don't miss the penguins at the Central Park Zoo. There's a good playground there too."
—Alex, 9, Chatham, NJ

10

Ground Zero

September 11, 2001 . . .

that's such a long time ago for kids! Maybe you weren't born yet.

But your parents and grandparents certainly remember that awful day.

We watched the images again and again of the hijacked planes hitting the World Trade Center and the buildings collapsing from the heat of the fires.

We thought a lot about the kids who lost a parent or an aunt or uncle. A lot of kids who weren't even born yet lost their dads. None of us can understand why someone would do something so terrible.

This event changed all of our lives. We realize that every time we stand in a long line and take off our shoes to go through security at airports.

Now more than 10 years later, we can go to the 9/11 Memorial and remember and honor those who were killed.

DID YOU KNOW?

George Washington was inaugurated near the location of the 9/11 Memorial on Wall and National Streets, not in Washington DC. Look for the Federal Hall National Memorial that marks the spot.

A NYC KID SAYS:

"My uncle was a fireman, and he died on 9/11. It was very sad because so many people died."
—Helen, 9, NYC

DID YOU KNOW?

The World Trade Center once included seven buildings. When the World Trade Center was built in 1973, the 110-story Twin Towers became the tallest buildings in the world. Some 50,000 people worked here—more people than live in many suburban towns!

It is beautiful, with two huge pools sitting in the original footprints of the Twin Towers—each is an acre—with huge waterfalls surrounding them.

You'll probably see kids from around the world here with their families. Everyone who visits New York wants to pay their respects.

When you get here, you're at the very bottom of Manhattan, the oldest part of New York City and the financial capital of the

WALLst

world. That's why the terrorists chose to attack the Twin Towers.

The **New York Stock Exchange** (www.nyse.com) and **Wall Street** are nearby. Many people work here, and many people live nearby too.

New Yorkers and the designers hope the new buildings will show the world how strong we all are.

A VISITING KID SAYS:
"Being here is a lot different than seeing it on TV. It makes it all much more real."
—Lindsey, 14, Clinton, NY

A NYC KID SAYS:
"I used to live downtown. My mom came and picked me up at school and took me to my cousins. We couldn't go home. My dad worked on the 56th floor, but he got out. I was really glad to see him. We couldn't go back to our house so we moved uptown."
—Hayley, 9, NYC

- It doesn't cost anything to visit the 9/11 Memorial, but because so many people want to visit, you've got to reserve free advance passes for a specific date and time. Check www.911memorial.org for more information. The website www.renew nyc.com talks about the rebuilding of Lower Manhattan.

- The 9/11 Memorial Museum will open in September 2012, a year after the memorial did. The museum will display artifacts associated with 9/11 and tell the stories of the people whose lives were imme-diately impacted by those events. You can find out more about the museum at www.911memorial .org/museum.

A NYC KID SAYS:
"It's important that we always remember the people who died here."
—Satesh, 9, Bronx, NY

When You Visit

Be prepared for security screening, just like at the airport. You can't bring a large backpack or a bag bigger than 8" x 17" x 19", animals (except service animals), glass bottles, skateboards, or weapons.

A VISITING KID SAYS:

"I like thinking about how important it was that people tried to save other people that day. It makes me feel sad, but it's good to come here with your family."
—Jessie, 8, Orlando, FL

DID YOU KNOW?

In 1664, the city's tallest structure was a 2-story windmill!

The Survivor Tree

A callery pear tree became known as the Survivor Tree after it lived through the September 11, 2001 terror attacks. It was discovered and freed from piles of rubble in the plaza of the World Trade Center and nursed back to health, despite a blackened trunk. It was planted at the memorial in December 2010 and hopefully will continue to grow among dozens of swamp white oak trees. When the memorial is complete, more than 400 trees will line the plaza—an urban forest!

A NYC KID SAYS:

"9/11 happened on the second day of school. It didn't seem real until I saw it on TV and visited Ground Zero. Some people say NYC isn't a community, but on 9/11 everyone was looking out for each other and trying to help. People were hugging strangers and crying."
—Amanda, 13, NYC

What a Trip!

I came to New York with:

_____

_____

_____

The weather was:

_____

_____

_____

We went to:

_____

_____

_____

We ate:

_____

_____

_____

We bought:

_____

_____

_____

I saw these famous New York sights:

_____

_____

_____

My favorite thing about New York was:

_____

_____

_____

My best memory of New York was:

_____

_____

_____

My favorite souvenir is:

_____

_____

_____

_____

_____

_____

You had such a great time in New York!!! Draw some pictures or paste in some photos of your trip!!!

Index

Algonquin Indians, 3
Alice in Wonderland, 103
Alphabet City, 12
Alvin Ailey American Dance
    Theater, 96
American Ballet Theatre, 96
American Folk Art Museum, 34
American Girl Place, 84
American Museum of Natural
    History, 26, 28, 30, 31, 34, 37, 105
Andersen, Hans Christian, 103
Apollo Theater, 22
art, 14, 26, 32, 33, 37
balloons, 86, 87
Balto the Dog, 104
baseball, 41, 47
basketball, 40, 46, 47, 85
Battery Park, 67, 69
Big Apple Circus, 61
Big Apple Greeter, 19
Bloomingdale's, 81
blue whale, 29
books, 20
boroughs, 5, 18, 23
Bronx, the, 5, 18, 105, 106
Bronx Zoo, 105, 106
Brooklyn, 5, 15, 18, 32, 34, 44, 51, 70,
    86, 95
Brooklyn Academy of Music, 95
Brooklyn Bridge, 15, 51, 70
Brooklyn Children's Museum, 32, 34
Brooklyn Cyclones, 44
Brooklyn Museum, 34
Carnegie Hall, 93
carousels, 42, 103
carriage rides, 100
Central Park, 27, 37, 46, 96, 99
Central Park Sailboats, 46
Central Park Zoo, 101, 105
checkers, 46
Chelsea, 12

Chelsea Piers Sports and
    Entertainment Complex, 16, 47
chess, 46
Children's Museum of Manhattan,
    32, 34
Chinatown, 12, 17, 80
Chrysler Building, 51, 52
Circle Line-Statue of Liberty Ferry, 69
Circle Line Tour, 51
circus, 61
Citi Field, 41
citizenship, 75
City of New York Parks and
    Recreation, 19
City Pass, 58
Cloisters, The, 32
Coney Island, 44
Conservatory Water, 46, 103
Costume Institute, 28
Dairy, The, 46, 100
Dance Theatre of Harlem, 22
dancing, 22, 47, 96
dinosaurs, 28, 30
Disney's New Amsterdam
    Theater, 57
Downtown Boathouse, 44
Dylan's Candy Bar, 84
Ellis Island, 66, 69
El Museo del Barrio, 34
Empire State Building, 50, 51, 55, 58
FAO Schwarz, 82
Federal Hall National Memorial, 110
Ferrara's, 83
Festival of San Gennaro, 83
firehouses, 9
Flatiron District, 13
food, 2, 14, 17, 22, 41, 52, 54, 58, 73,
    76, 80, 82, 83, 84, 88
football, 41
George Delacorte Musical Clock, 102
Good Morning America, 4, 58
Grand Central Terminal, 52, 86

Greenwich Village, 13, 16, 84
Ground Zero, 13, 109
Guggenheim Museum, 32, 34
Harlem, 14, 22
Harlem Meer, 46
Hayden Planetarium, 30
High Line, The, 17
history, 3, 33, 66, 70, 76, 82, 104, 115
hockey, 40, 41, 47
Hudson, Henry, 3
Hudson River, 16, 32, 42, 44
ice-skating, 44, 46, 47
immigrants, 18, 67, 68, 69, 77, 88
ING New York City Marathon, 45
Intrepid Sea, Air & Space
    Museum, 34
Jewish Museum, 35
Katz's Delicatessen, 88
kayaking, 44
languages, 2, 8, 59, 70, 80
Lincoln Center, 94
Little Italy, 14, 17, 82
Loeb Boathouse, 46
Lower East Side, 14, 17, 19, 77, 81, 88
Lower East Side Tenement Museum,
    17, 35, 89
Macy's Herald Square, 85
Macy's Thanksgiving Day Parade,
    53, 86, 87
Madame Tussaud's New York Wax
    Museum, 54
Madison Square Garden, 40, 41, 45
M&M's World, 54
Manhattan, 4, 5, 15, 18, 22, 32, 34,
    100, 112, 114
maps, 8
MetLife Stadium, 41, 43
MetroCard, 8
Metropolitan Museum of Art, The, 26,
    29, 35, 36, 37, 105
Metropolitan Opera, 96
Midtown, 14
movies, 21, 51, 106
mummies, 27, 29
Museum of Arts and Design, 35
Museum of Chinese in America, 82

Museum of Modern Art, The, 33, 35
Museum of the City of New York,
    33, 35
Museum of the Moving Image in
    Queens, 35
museums, 25, 34, 85
music, 6, 22, 91, 105
name of New York, 3
Nassau Veterans Memorial
    Coliseum, 40
National Museum of the American
    Indian, 33, 35
National September 11 Memorial,
    110, 112, 114
NBA Store, 85
neighborhoods, 5, 9, 11, 23
New Jersey Devils, 41
New Jersey Nets, 40
New Museum, 35
New York Botanical Garden, 45
New York City Ballet, 96
New York City Fire Museum, 15
New York Giants, 41, 43
New York Islanders, 41
New York Jets, 41, 43
New York Knicks, 40, 45
New York Liberty, The, 40
New York Mets, 41, 43
New York Pass, 58
New York Public Library, 63
New York Rangers, 40, 45
New York Stock Exchange, 113
New York Transit Museum, 86
New York Transit Museum in
    Brooklyn, 86
New York Yankees, 41, 43, 45
9/11 Memorial Museum, 114
Nolita, 14
North Meadow Recreation Center, 46
Nutcracker, 95
Paley Center for Media, The, 35
parks, 19
playgrounds, 9, 19, 101, 102
Prudential Center, 41
public transportation, 6, 53, 86
puppet shows, 105

Queens, 5, 18, 35, 41, 61
Radio City Music Hall, 53
Radio City Rockettes, 53, 87
Ringling Brothers Barnum & Bailey Circus, 61
Rockefeller Center, 4, 44, 53, 60
Rockefeller Center Ice Rink, 44
Rockefeller Center Tree, 60
rocks, 29
Roof Garden, 37
Ruby Foo's, 85
Sheep Meadow, 102
shopping, 14, 17, 19, 22, 36, 54, 57, 76, 80, 81, 82, 85, 88
skatepark, 42
SoHo, 14, 17, 84
Sony Wonder Technology Lab, 85
South Street Seaport, 76, 96
South Street Seaport Museum, 76
souvenirs, 54, 57
sports, 16, 39
Staten Island, 5, 13, 18, 74
Statue of Liberty, 51, 66, 73, 74
Strawberry Fields, 102
street vendors, 2, 54, 57, 77, 84
subways, 6, 53, 81, 86, 92

Survivor Tree, 116
Swedish Cottage Marionette Theatre, 105
taxis, 8, 19
Temple of Dendur, 27
tennis, 40
theater, 15, 54, 57
Time Out New York Kids, 19
Times Square, 15, 53, 55, 58
Today Show, The, 4, 58
Toys "R" Us, 57
TriBeCa, 15
Unicorn Tapestries, 33
United Nations, The, 62
Upper East Side, 16
Upper West Side, 16
US Open Tennis Championship, 40
Victorian Gardens, 101
Wall Street, 113
Washington, George, 6, 37, 110
Washington Square Park, 16, 93
weapons, 28
Wollman Rink, 46, 101
World Trade Center, 13, 109
Yankee Stadium, 41

WORD SEARCH
ANSWER KEY:

```
S T S M U X O M D S D X Y R J E N
T I O A A H E M S N T L W K G T B
A M T N J L S G P Y A B Z A D H R
T E G H R V O W F T V L L W J E O
E S K A Q T H P I W R L S N Z B O
N S H T Z M O E E J I B D I O R K
I Q I T J H L S F V X Y N S N O L
S U E A Z T L R H H R L X R T N Y
L A V N T E K C Z V T G H L R X N
A R E I W K I G R O U N D Z E R O
N E L E X W Z E A F O H R N N X J
D M R E N E D I S M I D T O W N Q
H I H E M C H I N A T O W N E Q U
C T E V L O W E R E A S T S I D E
G R N T R C L W T X N V U H Q W E
G K T D T R I B E C A Q I M X O N
U N S P U O D W K B R N S F B R S
```

About the Author

Award-winning author Eileen Ogintz is a leading national family travel expert whose syndicated "Taking the Kids" is the most widely distributed column in the country on family travel. She has also created TakingtheKids.com, which helps families to make the most of their vacations together. Ogintz is the author of seven family travel books and is often quoted in major publications such as *USA Today*, the *Wall Street Journal*, and the *New York Times*, as well as parenting and women's magazines on family travel. She has appeared on such television programs as *The Today Show*, *Good Morning America*, and *The Oprah Winfrey Show*, as well as dozens of local radio and television news programs. She has traveled around the world with her three children and others in the family, talking to other traveling families wherever she goes.